Smart Outsourcing from A to Z

◆

How to Save Millions and Increase Growth for any Business in 90 days

Joshua Keith Cook

www.ThinkingLeaders.com

Preface

Human resource (HR) outsourcing is a very popular choice for small to medium sized businesses. This method of HR outsourcing has proven to be an effective mechanism to reduce costs and increase market share. Many businesses have decided to become one hundred percent paperless, tossing out their big filing cabinets, fax, and copy machines. They have upgraded to a new digital world of virtual HR systems that use modern tools, such as user-friendly online databases that can be accessed through smart phones, tablets, and laptops. These innovative companies are saving millions and are implementing more efficient methods of streamlining HR processes. Outsourced HR functions keep companies focused on what matters most and helps teams become more productive and profitable.

SMART OUTSOURCING FROM A to Z

Dedications

---◆---

I would like to dedicate this book to my son
Nolan. May he never stop learning
throughout his journey in life.

Contents

SMART OUTSOURCING FROM A to Z

CHAPTER 1

What is Smart Outsourcing ?

"We become what we behold…we shape our tools, and thereafter our tools shape us."

Marshall McLuhan

What is the purpose of studying business philosophy and business best practices? What is the goal or end game? The goal of most business leaders throughout the centuries has been exploring what methodologies and business models really work. This book will point innovative leaders in the right direction to take their company to the next level. Leaders will think differently by exploring what questions successful business leaders have been grappling with throughout the centuries: how to reduce costs, how to increase market share, how to grow their customer base, and how to reduce customer

churn. Leaders must apply these nuances

and wise insights to modern business

challenges and opportunities.

Thinking differently and understanding the

business environment and understanding

how other people have thought in the past

will give successful leaders the edge to make

key decisions and judgments they have to

face from day to day. Today's leaders need

the right business philosophy to know how

to communicate well with people in

management, and in how to sell to

consumers. Leaders must reduce costs,

effectively streamline processes and add more value for its customers. This book is a road map for developing a new world view and provides a unique approach to outsourcing in today's business environment. This book is also an important reference to go back to for any leader who wants a new innovative approach to finding real growth opportunities for their companies.

CHAPTER 2

Human Resource Outsourcing:

How winning small businesses think big and save smart

"Real thinking is hard –not only laborious but more often than not unsuccessful, leaving us with a frustrating sense of our own inadequacy and our ignorance, not to mention exposing these to raised eyebrows of others."

-Bryan Magee

Contemporary companies are constantly finding new ways and approaches to make operational and other processes more efficient and cost effective. Many companies are choosing to outsource different functions in their organizations, and one of those functions is outsourcing human resource processes.

For many traditional executives, outsourcing HR functions is a daunting idea; for other leaders it's liberating. While some companies still feel the need to retain their human resource department because they continue to want to maintain face-to-face contact with their employees, many companies are outsourcing their human resource functions and are hiring HR generalists or assistants to manage the relationships with outsourced vendors.

Many companies are outsourcing their human resource department to increase value, efficiency, and reduce costs. Another important reason companies outsource is they want to hire specialized professionals to perform certain complex projects. For example, if a firm is small, they may outsource a project to redesign a pension system for their employees.

As with increased efficiency, cost is a very important aspect in today's economy, and companies are trying to find drastic ways to save money, but not at the expense of cutting value for their employees. Many companies are outsourcing HR processes to a human resource consulting firm or hiring a professional employer organization (PEO) because they can significantly reduce costs and add more value within the organization.

For many organizations, the goals of HR outsourcing are to:

- Contain HR costs
- Reduce administrative burden
- Minimize employer-related risk
- Create value for existing employees

Why should HR functions be outsourced?

Business leaders did not enter into business to manage human resource functions. The pivotal focus for most business leaders is to discover innovative ideas to improve market share, find better strategies of winning over their competition, and increase customer loyalty.

"Many companies are outsourcing their human resource department to increase value, efficiency, and reduce costs."

HUMAN RESOURCE OUTSOURCING

Human resource management functions on the other hand can be complex, requiring adequate time, energy, and resources to handle in-house. Processing these functions must also be handled correctly and efficiently. They include:

- benefits planning
- recruiting
- training
- managing personnel files
- payroll
- performance reviews
- managing leaves

- other HR administration issues

Managing third party vendors

Another challenge of managing HR functions in-house is managing multiple third party vendor relationships. Company administrators need to manage a payroll vendor, tax authorities, health insurance brokers, health insurance carriers, voluntary benefits, recruiters, compensation data, employee policies, outplacement, legal guidance, and many other vendors.

When it comes to benefits, many small businesses lack negotiating leverage. Small businesses don't have negotiating power when dealing with large insurance carriers and other vendors. The result is the lack of control over escalating costs related to employee benefits.

When customizing an effective human resource outsourcing strategy, it is essential to first understand the company's goals and vision. Developing a plan to outsource human resource functions requires strategic planning to establish the right scope and implementation to produce the desired results for return on investment.

Options to process HR functions

- DIY: Do it Yourself
- Multi-vendor Solution
- Professional Employer Organization

Companies have three basic options to

process certain HR functions. First,

companies can do it themselves and build an

in-house human resource department. The

upside is companies control everything, but

the downside is companies don't have the

time to do it all, nor do companies want the

liability of making costly mistakes through

human error, missing deadlines or non-

compliance with federal or state laws.

Business leaders need to focus on other priorities to grow the business.

Second, another option is the multi-vendor solution in which some companies decide to outsource to multiple vendors. They may choose one vendor for each specific task and area of expertise such as payroll and benefits. The upside is companies can get experts to do the work, which saves the company from doing HR administration tasks. The downside according to a study by Price Waterhouse Cooper, organizations using multiple vendors for payroll and HR-related services can spend more than $100 US per employee per year just to integrate these processes and providers. This cost represents close to six percent of total HR and payroll budgets. Because of the cost of multiple vendors, many companies are making a bold move towards a single vendor or PEO.

The third option is the use of a Professional Employer Organization (PEO) as a single vendor HRO solution. Many companies get increased efficiencies, an improved employment brand image, and a renewed ability to focus on the core business. The upside is companies can manage a single relationship and gain HR expertise, the newest HR technology, and a qualified team to manage company HR functions.

Choosing the right vendor

It is imperative to choose the right PEO, HR consulting firm, or HR vendor. There are a few things company leaders should consider when planning to choose an HR vendor. First, company leaders need to look at the vendor's financial strength and quality of service. Second, the vendor needs to be flexible in pricing and fair in negotiating the contract or service agreement. Third, the vendor must be flexible with changes that the company will face as they grow or downsize.

"Single vendor solutions provide companies with increased efficiencies, and the ability to focus on core business."

Negotiating the contract and pricing agreements

Daniel R. Mummery, Esq., a partner in the law firm, Latham & Watkins' Silicon Valley, states that negotiating a HR outsourcing agreement requires one to first understand the relevant business issues. He explains, "The key components of some service contracts should cover: statements of work, pricing details, service-level agreements (SLAs), a transition plan, governance requirements, and an exit plan."

HR outsourcing has proven to improve human resource functions in streamlining and managing daily tasks for administrators, dramatically cutting costs, improving the company's bottom line, and adding value for employees which effects the company's ability to retain and attract top talent.

Outsourcing HR consultants can save organizations massive amounts of money by keeping leaders up to speed in an ever changing environment. HR professionals also help companies meet the challenges in a changing world by adopting and implementing the best human resources philosophies and methodology.

Say No to Form Pollution!

Many sales organizations, from car dealerships to software companies, have some methods of tracking their goals and sales. Some leaders are particularly obsessed with numbers, forms, spreadsheets, white boards, posters, signs, digital gadgets all to perform the same task and function. The danger of using all this data and ways to track different metrics is that communication becomes redundant and loses its effect on goals, production and creativity. What is worse than pollution? Music can be great, but when one plays multiple songs at the same time, the music loses its enjoyment and becomes annoying noise to the listener. This is the same effect with too many forms, sales metrics, and goals to the sales team. When leaders demand sales teams to compile too many numerous forms of data, it becomes very tedious, redundant, and lacks any meaning, nor does it motivate. The process becomes a task instead of a tool.

Tools are made to help teams succeed in tasks, motivate and coach. Many frontline employees feel punished when they are given tasks to fill out forms with information that they already have. Leaders can keep a few concepts in mind when developing winning teams pertaining to forms, sales goals and sales metrics.

Leaders hire sales staff for their expertise. If leaders want someone to fill out forms and spreadsheets all day, they need to outsource this process to an office assistant. Successful leaders hire skilled professionals who are passionate about selling; therefore, successful leaders do not demotivate employees by giving their people clip boards and sticky notes.

Leaders must empower members of teams as unique individual leaders. As the philosopher Martin Heidegger so aptly highlighted, humans are not machines or computers, but unique beings. Humans are designed to be aware of their own experiences, and to treat them as robots is a futile task that is ineffective.

Leaders should coach teams to success not by making the focal point all about numbers and metrics, but by teaching employees the correct behaviors to exhibit. If the behaviors and actions exist, results will come.

Here are three secrets to team success:

- Goal Setting
- Give Real Time Coaching Feedback
- Show them what "Right" looks like

Goal setting is imperative for team success, but many leaders do all the talking and make imperative statements, jot down some notes, and bid sales professionals a good day. Successful leaders will have sales professionals design their unique strategies to succeed. Leaders may then ask questions to help sales professionals exceed their goals. Leaders need to find out their sales professional's goals, dreams, and whether these sales professionals want to be promoted with the reward of making more money. Do these professionals want to make a 100K salary, do they have daily strategies to achieve these goals?

Leaders must give real time coaching feedback. Leaders must give encouragement and let employees know that they are doing a great job and ask them to do it again. When sales professionals make mistakes or fall short, what is the approach? Leaders must show employees "what right looks like" and hold them accountable. Sales professionals should be given the tools to be successful. After leaders have communicated the team's tasks and empowered the team to lead the organization, leaders must be involved with their teams. The leader should make his or her own goal each day, committing to helping team members who need help the most and add value to the identified sales professional's day. Leaders must insure not to duplicate themselves. Leaders should challenge employees to become better by using their own unique talents and reinvent themselves to become excellent knowledge workers. The idea of "existence precedes essence," which Jean Sartre coined, means humans are free to choose whom they want to become. Humans are not pre-programmed machines who have no real choices in life. They are determined to be free. Therefore, leaders should encourage their team to flourish into what is possible; a team without vision can never be a "dream team!"

CHAPTER **4**

Danka on Courage and Innovation

"Have the courage to turn ideas into action."

Danka, a copier sales company, cut costs by eliminating their HR staff and outsourced their entire HR process to TriNet.[1] They cut their HR cost by as much as 50%. TriNet came in and trained their leaders to use a self-service platform. An interesting highlighted feature is their 100% paperless systems. Small businesses no longer need to purchase massive file cabinets or copiers. By eliminating their HR department, organizations will be able to utilize TriNet's

---

[1] Rosenthal, 2006.

benefits, like 401K, actually adding more value for their employees.

Outsourcing HR functions only worked for Danka, because they were willing to embrace change and met for 30 minutes every week with TriNet staff during the transition. Keith Nelson, Danka's Chief Administrative Officer, had two goals in mind, to turn his company around by cutting costs and producing efficiencies. Meredith Johnson, RVP for TriNet, helped Nelson with his goals, and together they analyzed every aspect of their HR spending. They were able to cut out unnecessary spending and agreed on a service-level agreement (SLAs) that was a good fit for Danka. Now Nelson calls Johnson his "VP of HR". [2]

Contemporary companies are constantly finding new ways and approaches to make operational and other processes more efficient and cost effective. Many companies are choosing to outsource different functions in their organizations, and one of those functions is outsourcing human resource processes.

---

[2] Rosenthal, 2006.

"Play up your strengths and delegate your weakness."

Donald Trump,
The Art of the Deal.

CHAPTER **5**

Putting Theory into Action

"We are what we
repeatedly do.
Excellence, then,
is a habit."
                Socrates

In order for leaders to be successful, they must be brave enough to make tough decisions and judgment calls. Leaders need to embrace change and develop a new model of doing business by taking inventory of their costs and re-examining their work processes and procedures. Leaders must take action to reduce waste and ineffective processes.

Knowledge is one of the greatest commodities in today's business environment, but applied knowledge and being brave enough to drive knowledge will be a leader's watershed moment.

Outsourcing HR functions is one of the options business leaders are taking to make a big impact for organizational success. Leaders will be faced with tough decisions and will face criticism, but where there is risk, there is also reward. The leaders who are innovative and who are willing to take new approaches will succeed in the future.

Top HR Vendors Directory from A to Z

Absalom Systems International

Accenture Ltd

ADP (Automatic Data Processing, Inc.)

Affiliated Computer Services, Inc.

Aon Corporation

Ascentis Corporation

Askari Information Systems Limited

ASL Enterprises Inc.

Aspiration

Atlas Business Solutions, Inc.

Authoria, Inc.

Automatic Data Processing Inc.

Auxillium West

Beakware Stylus Systems Pvt. Ltd.

Bluechip Computer Consultants Pvt. Ltd.

Cascade HR Ltd.

Ceridian Corporation

Cezanne Software

CheckPoint HR LLC

CompuPay, Inc.

Computers In Personnel

ComSpec International, Inc.

Concur Technologies Inc.

Convergys Corporation

Copraxis

Cornerstone OnDemand, Inc.

Cort Software Inc.

Creative Software Pvt. Ltd.

CWS Software

Cyberaid Pty. Ltd.

Delphi Software

Deltek, Inc.

DenoSys LLC

Dytech Group, Inc.

E-chex, Inc. Payroll Solutions

e-HRpro

EBenefits Solutions

Empagio, Inc.

Employease Inc.

EmployeeConnect Pty Ltd

Eugenisys, Inc.

Excel HRM

ExcellerateHRO Corporation

First Advantage

First Reference Inc.

Fiserv Inc.

Fluous Solutions Pvt. Ltd.

FMR Corp.

Genesys Software Systems, Inc.

Gevity HR, Inc.

Glovia International, Inc.

Halogen Software, Inc.

Hewitt Associates, Inc.

High Line Corp.

Houston Technologies Limited

HR-ease

HR3

HRMS Solutions Inc.

HRN Management Group

hSenid Software International (Pvt.) Ltd.

Human Resources MicroSystems

Humanic Design

Hurstridge Technologies

iEmployee

IFS

Infor Global Solutions

Ingentra HR Services Inc.

Innovative Employee Solutions

Institute for Corporate Productivity

Integral Systems Inc.

Intelligo Software Ltd. Inc.

International Business Machines Corp.

Intuit Inc.

J. J. Keller & Associates, Inc.

Jenss & Associates

Jenzabar, Inc.

JSM Technologies Pvt. Ltd

Kenexa Corporation

Kronos Incorporated

Laserbeam Software

Lawson Software, Inc.

Mangrove Software Inc.

Maxumise Consulting Pty. Ltd.

Meta4 Groupe ADONIX

Microsoft Corporation

Midland HR

MyPayrollHR.com

MyStaff Pty. Ltd.

Neterson Technologies Pvt. Ltd.

NetPay Payroll

NetSimplicity

NetTeam Management Solutions

Nisus NV

Norchard Solutions Ltd.

NorthgateArinso

NuView, Inc.

Odin HR Technology

Open4

Oracle CorporationOrange

Digital Systems Inc.

OrangeHRM Inc.

Paychex Inc.

PayChoice

PayCycle, Inc.

PayGlobal Pty. Ltd.

Payroll Professionals, Inc.

PDS, Inc.PerfectSoftware Inc.

Perquest

Plateau Systems Ltd.

PPI (Payroll People, Inc.)

PrimePay Inc

PSTek

QHR Software Inc.

Ramco Systems Corporation

Replicon Inc.

Sage Software, Inc.

SAP Aktiengesellschaft

Security Management Consulting Inc.

Sentient Inc.

ServerVault Corp.

SharedHR

Simply Personnel

Smartree Ltd.

Snowdrop Systems Ltd.

SourceOne Payroll Services

Spectrum Human Resource Systems Corp.

StepStone Solution

SunGard Data Systems Inc.

SurePayroll

Taleo Corp.

Technical Difference Inc.

Technology One Limited

The Ultimate Software Group, Inc.

TimePlus Payroll

Trak-It Solutions Inc.

Trigon Road LLC

TriNet Group

TUT Services Inc.

UCN Inc.

UnicornHRO

Vizual Business Tools PLC

Vurv Technology

Workscape Inc.

Podcasts

Talking HR Podcast

Success Factors' People Performance
Radio Personnel Today Audio

Public Sector HR Podcast

Jim Stroud's Recruiters Lounge

Workforce Innovations

APQC's HCM podcast

TV's Successful HR Strategies

Ceridian's HR and Payroll podcast

Resources

Selected Quotes

"Only buy something that you'd be perfectly happy to hold if the market shut down for 10 years." Warren Buffett

"Well, yes, I've fired a lot of people. Generally I like other people to fire, because it's always a lousy task. But I have fired many people." Donald Trump

"Remember, a real decision is measured by the fact that you've taken new action. If there's no action, you haven't truly decided." Anthony Robbins

"Each Wal-Mart store should reflect the values of its customers and support the vision they hold for their community." Sam Walton

"Most people struggle with life balance simply because they haven't paid the price to decide what is really important to them." Stephen Covey

"A lot of people are afraid to tell the truth, to say no. That's where toughness comes into play. Toughness is not being a bully. It's having backbone." Robert Kiyosaki

"Ridiculous yachts and private planes and big limousines won't make people enjoy life more, and it sends out terrible messages to the people who work for them. It would be so much better if that money was spent in Africa – and it's about getting a balance." Richard Branson

"I have found no greater satisfaction than achieving success through honest dealing and strict adherence to the view that, for you to gain, those you deal with should gain as well." Alan Greenspan

"We provide food that customers love, day after day after day. People just want more of it." Ray Kroc

"Willingness to change is a strength, even if it means plunging part of the company into total confusion for a while." Jack Welch

"A warrior of light who trusts too much in his intelligence will end up underestimating the power of his opponent."
Paulo Coelho

"Executives owe it to the organization and to their fellow workers not to tolerate nonperforming individuals in important jobs."
Peter Drucker

"Money made through dishonest practices will not last long."
Chinese Proverbs

"To turn really interesting ideas and fledgling technologies into a company that can continue to innovate for years, it requires a lot of disciplines."
Steve Jobs

References

ADP (2010). Retrieved February 22, 2010. http://adp.com/about-us.aspx

Cook, Joshua (2011) How Winning Small Business Think Big and Save Smart. Retrieved: http://www.drakepulse.com/index.php/2011/03/09/how-winning-small-businesses-think-big-save-smart/

Lendino, Jamie (2006). Outsourcing can grow your business. Retrieved March 3, 2010. http://www.cnet.com/4520-10192_1-6411746-1.html

Miller, Stephen (2005). Study: Benefits Outsourcing Can Save Money, Increase Efficiencies. Retrieved February 23, 2010.

http://www.shrm.org/hrdisciplin
es/Pages/CMS_012654

Noe, (2010). Human Resource
Management. McGraw-Hill
Irwin. New York, NY. Pg 733.

Rosenthal, Beth (2006). How to
Outsource Everything in HR.
Retrieved February 22, 2010.
http://www.shrm.org/hrdisciplin
es/Pages/CMS_018010.aspx

TriNet (2010), Alarm Central
saves time and finds expertise
with TriNet. Retrieved
http://www.trinet.com/document
s/case_studies/CS_Alarm_Centr
al.pdf

Smart Outsourcing from A-Z

About the Author

Joshua Cook currently lives with his wife and son in Travelers Rest, SC. He is currently a sales manager. Joshua Cook graduated with a BA from Southeastern University. He will graduate in 2012 with a MBA from North Greenville University.

Current Highlights:

Joshua Cook has been published in *Drake Business Review* and is an expert author for EZINES.com. Joshua has written five books: *Extreme Power, Smart Outsourcing from A to Z, The Fifth Imperative, The Ethics of Euthyphro: Piety, Justice, and Love.*

Philosophy:

The purpose of *Smart Outsourcing from A to Z* is to promote and inspire the best thoughts and ideas in the topic of leadership for business professionals who are interested in leadership development. My desire is for the contents of this book to be thought provoking and life changing. For more resources, please visit my blog for free resources and see my other books at: www.ThinkingLeaders.com.

Contact Information

Prizm Marketing Group LLC

864.660.9583

josh@thinkingleaders.com

www.ThinkingLeaders.com

INDEX

Smart Outsourcing from A to Z

How to Save Millions and Increase Growth for any Business in 90 days

PLEASE VISIT OUR WEBSITE FOR FREE RESOURCES

www.ThinkingLeaders.com